ROBERT. M. DRAKE

SCIENCE.

THE STARS IN ME ARE THE STARS IN YOU.

SHE WAS MOVED BY EVERYTHING AND SHE WAS BEAUTIFUL. NO WORDS COULD EVER DEFINE THE TYPE OF LOVE SHE IMAGINED FOR HERSELF.

SOCIETY TAUGHT US HOW TO HATE. HATE TAUGHT US VIOLENCE. VIOLENCE TAUGHT US REGRET. REGRET TAUGHT US PAIN. PAIN TAUGHT US LOVE. LOVE TAUGHT US HOW TO LAUGH AND LAUGHTER MAKES EVERY MOMENT FAR MORE BEAUTIFUL THEN WE COULD EVER IMAGINE.

MAGIC IS WHEN YOU LIVE YOUR LIFE THE WAY YOU DIDN'T PICTURE IT AND LEAVE NOTHING BEHIND.

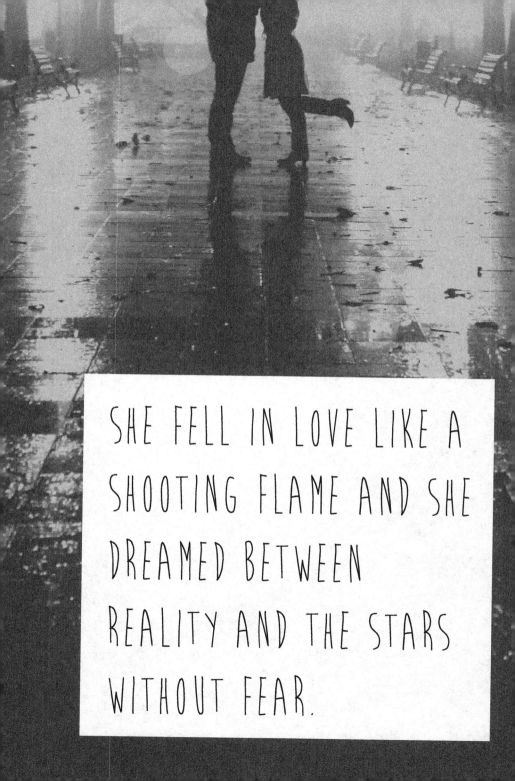

SHE FELL IN LOVE LIKE A SHOOTING FLAME AND SHE DREAMED BETWEEN REALITY AND THE STARS WITHOUT FEAR.

THE WORLD HATED HER
BECAUSE THEY COULDN'T
UNDERSTAND THE SCIENCE
THAT MADE HER ALL THAT
SHE WAS.

THE THINGS WE DON'T
TALK ABOUT ARE USUALLY
DISGUISED PASSIONS WE
AREN'T SUITED FOR.

MADNESS AND CHAOS ARE SELF-DESTRUCTING BUT OVER THINKING IS THE SUICIDE.

YOU AND ME,
THE WILD AIR,
THE NAKED TREES,
JUST THE MOON AND
NOT A SOUL TO
INTERRUPT.

EXHAUST YOURSELF, DREAM
DREAMS DEEP INTO THE
DEEPEST DREAMS AND ESCAPE
THE HORROR OF REALITY, WITH
A SHADOWY BEAUTY INTO THE
WILDERNESS, WHERE ALL
DREAMS ARE BORN.

SHE WAS BROKEN FROM MOMENT TO
MOMENT, WATCHING HER WORLD
COLLIDE SHE FELT LOST INSIDE
HERSELF. SHE FELL APART FOR A
PASSION THAT FLAMED BENEATH HER.
SHE WAITED AND DIED A HUNDRED
TIMES, IT DRIPPED FROM HER PORES.
THE MOMENT SHE LET GO, SHE
SOARED OVER THE STILLNESS LIKE
THE STAR SHE WAS BORN TO BE.

THE TRUTH IS I DIDN'T NEED THERAPY; I JUST NEEDED TO FEEL LOVED AND KNOW THAT SOMEONE OUT THERE CRAVED MY ATTENTION.

THAT NIGHT I DIDN'T SAY ANYTHING. I JUST WATCHED YOU LEAVE AND IN THE END, I JUST STAYED SLEEPING AWAKE. SOMEWHERE BETWEEN A SWEET DREAM AND A BEAUTIFUL NIGHTMARE, HOPING ONE DAY YOU'D RETURN TO RID ME OF THE DEMONS YOU LEFT BEHIND.

A TAMED WOMAN
WILL NEVER LEAVE
HER MARK IN THE
WORLD.

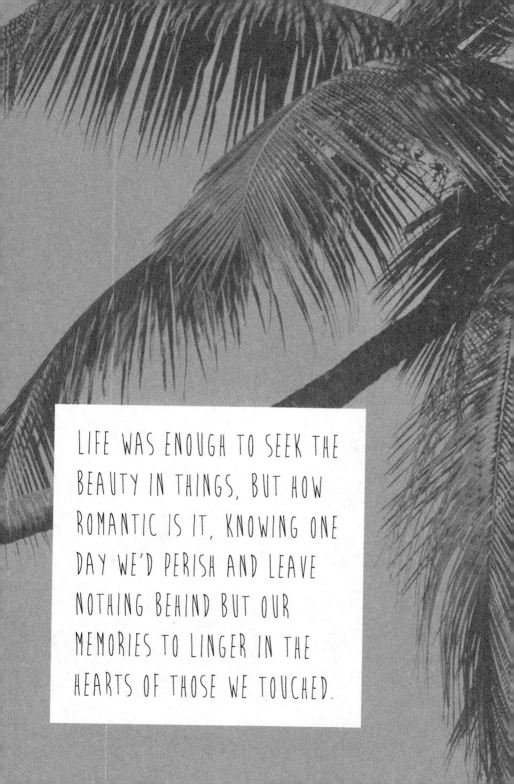

LIFE WAS ENOUGH TO SEEK THE BEAUTY IN THINGS, BUT HOW ROMANTIC IS IT, KNOWING ONE DAY WE'D PERISH AND LEAVE NOTHING BEHIND BUT OUR MEMORIES TO LINGER IN THE HEARTS OF THOSE WE TOUCHED.

THE GREATEST ADVENTURE
IS TO HAVE NO FEAR FOR
THE BLAZE THAT LIES AHEAD.

HATE ME ALL YOU WANT, FOR HATE ARE ALL THE THINGS YOU DESIRE BUT HAVE NOT.

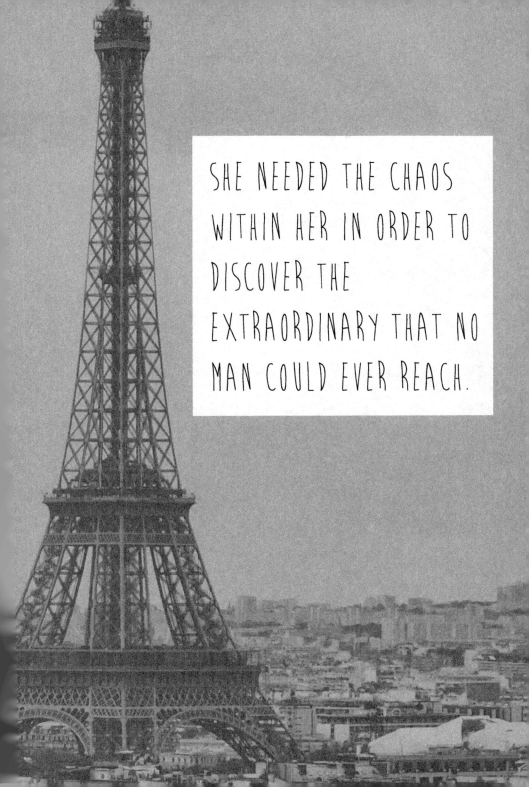

SHE NEEDED THE CHAOS WITHIN HER IN ORDER TO DISCOVER THE EXTRAORDINARY THAT NO MAN COULD EVER REACH.

IT WAS A DYING ART
THE WAY HE STAYED
AWAKE WATCHING HER
DREAM UNDERNEATH
THE STARS.

ART BREEDS LOVE,
YET ART IS BIRTHED
BY PAIN.

SHE WASN'T BROKEN;
SHE WAS JUST BENT
OVER THE CHANCE OF
BEING IGNORED BY
THE ONE SHE LOVED.

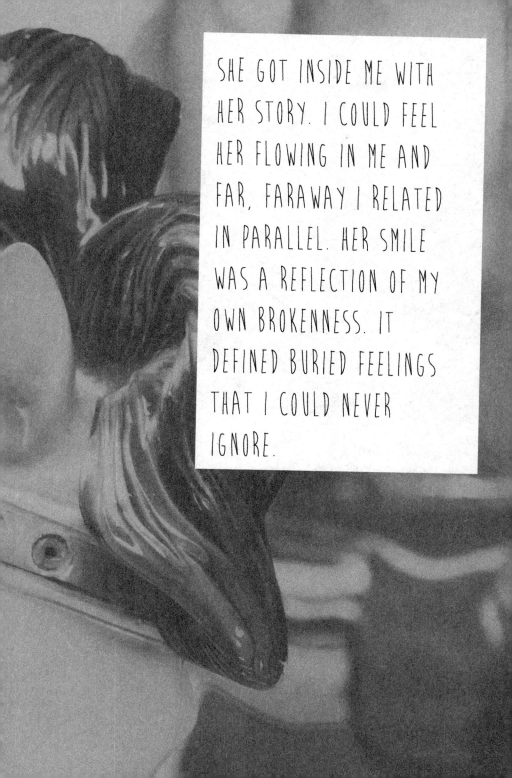

SHE GOT INSIDE ME WITH HER STORY. I COULD FEEL HER FLOWING IN ME AND FAR, FARAWAY I RELATED IN PARALLEL. HER SMILE WAS A REFLECTION OF MY OWN BROKENNESS. IT DEFINED BURIED FEELINGS THAT I COULD NEVER IGNORE.

MAYBE ONE DAY WE'LL FIND
THAT PLACE, WHERE YOU
AND I COULD BE TOGETHER
AND WE'LL CATCH OUR
DREAMS WITHIN THE WAVES
OF CHANGE. SO HEAR ME,
YOU ARE NOT ALONE.

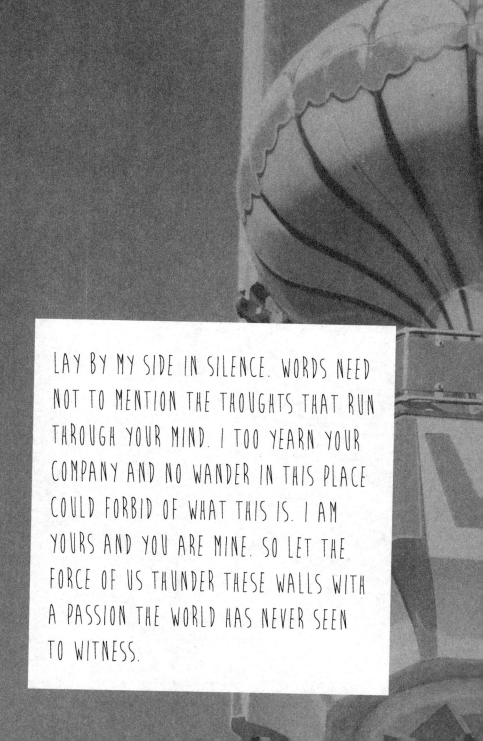

LAY BY MY SIDE IN SILENCE. WORDS NEED NOT TO MENTION THE THOUGHTS THAT RUN THROUGH YOUR MIND. I TOO YEARN YOUR COMPANY AND NO WANDER IN THIS PLACE COULD FORBID OF WHAT THIS IS. I AM YOURS AND YOU ARE MINE. SO LET THE FORCE OF US THUNDER THESE WALLS WITH A PASSION THE WORLD HAS NEVER SEEN TO WITNESS.

I NEED YOU BECAUSE I KNOW I
DESERVE YOU BUT LET ME FALL
IN LOVE WITH YOU ONE LAST
TIME BEFORE I LET GO. SO I
CAN REMEMBER THE BEAUTIFUL
IMPERFECTION THAT RATTLED
MY BONES.

WE ARE THE SOCIETY WE SO
DESPERATELY BLAME FOR ALL
OUR FAULTS BURIED BENEATH
OUR SCARS.

USE LOVE AS THE ONLY INSTRUMENT
TO QUESTION THE WORLD AROUND YOU.

WE ALL NEED LOVE; GOD JUST HIDES IT IN THE MOST UNUSUAL PLACES. SO FIND ITS SPARKLE AND LET IT WAVE THROUGH THE BREATH OF NEW BEGINNINGS.

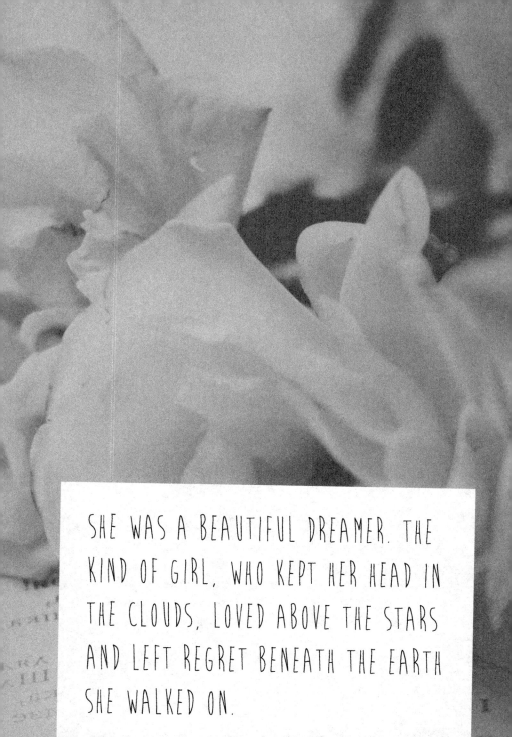

SHE WAS A BEAUTIFUL DREAMER. THE KIND OF GIRL, WHO KEPT HER HEAD IN THE CLOUDS, LOVED ABOVE THE STARS AND LEFT REGRET BENEATH THE EARTH SHE WALKED ON.

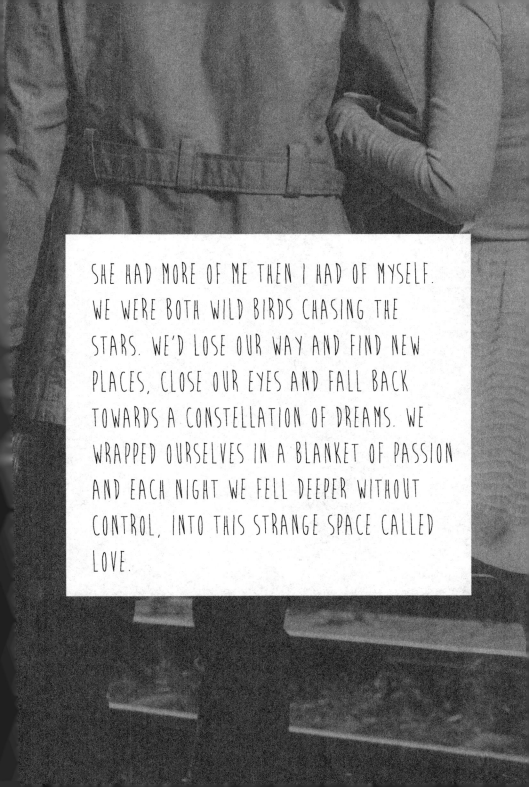

SHE HAD MORE OF ME THEN I HAD OF MYSELF.
WE WERE BOTH WILD BIRDS CHASING THE
STARS. WE'D LOSE OUR WAY AND FIND NEW
PLACES, CLOSE OUR EYES AND FALL BACK
TOWARDS A CONSTELLATION OF DREAMS. WE
WRAPPED OURSELVES IN A BLANKET OF PASSION
AND EACH NIGHT WE FELL DEEPER WITHOUT
CONTROL, INTO THIS STRANGE SPACE CALLED
LOVE.

WITH ALL HONESTY, SOMEWHERE
BETWEEN THE HELLO AND THE
DREAMS I SAW YOU IN I FELL
IN LOVE.

I KEPT LOVING AND LOVING AND LOVING.
EVERY WAKING HOUR, I MARVELED ON HOW
THESE MOMENTS WOULD MAKE MADE ME FEEL.
I WANTED TO LOVE THE WORLD AND BE THE
CHANGE IT SO DELICIOUSLY CRAVED.

IT WAS NEVER ABOUT THE WORLD BEING TOO
BIG, IT WAS MORE LIKE SHE WAS TOO MUCH
FOR THE WORLD TO HANDLE.

WE'RE ONLY INSTRUMENTS OF LOVE, FLOWING THROUGH HEAPS OF PAIN HOPING ONE DAY WE'D HATCH A PASSION OF OUR OWN.

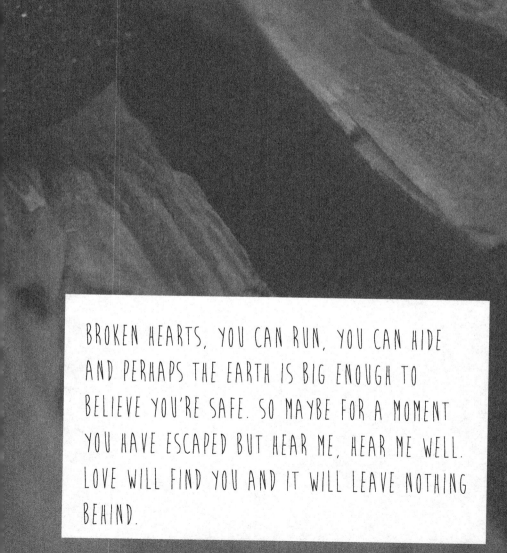

BROKEN HEARTS, YOU CAN RUN, YOU CAN HIDE
AND PERHAPS THE EARTH IS BIG ENOUGH TO
BELIEVE YOU'RE SAFE. SO MAYBE FOR A MOMENT
YOU HAVE ESCAPED BUT HEAR ME, HEAR ME WELL.
LOVE WILL FIND YOU AND IT WILL LEAVE NOTHING
BEHIND.

APPRECIATE THE MOMENT OF A
FIRST KISS; IT MAY BE THE LAST
TIME YOU OWN YOUR HEART.

MAYBE LOVE WAS MEANT TO SAVE US FROM OURSELVES.

SHE HAD THE POWER TO CHANGE THE WORLD BUT SHE COULDN'T SAVE THE ONE SHE LOVED.

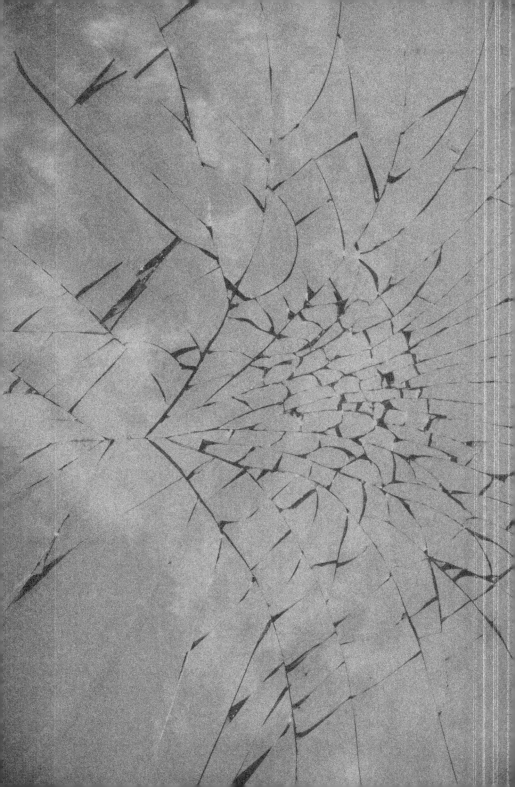

SOMETIMES THE MOST
BEAUTIFUL PEOPLE ARE
BEAUTIFULLY BROKEN.

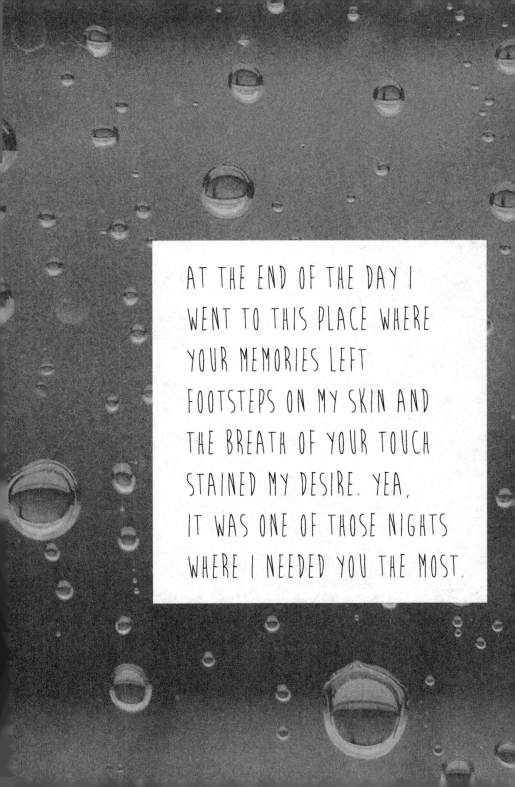

AT THE END OF THE DAY I
WENT TO THIS PLACE WHERE
YOUR MEMORIES LEFT
FOOTSTEPS ON MY SKIN AND
THE BREATH OF YOUR TOUCH
STAINED MY DESIRE. YEA,
IT WAS ONE OF THOSE NIGHTS
WHERE I NEEDED YOU THE MOST.

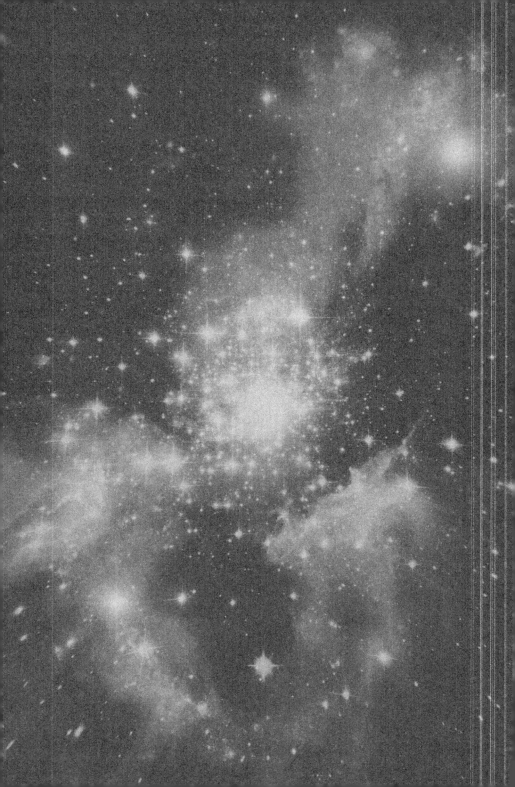

WE SWALLOWED THE CHAOS
BECAUSE WE KNEW WE DIDN'T
WANT TO BE ORDINARY.

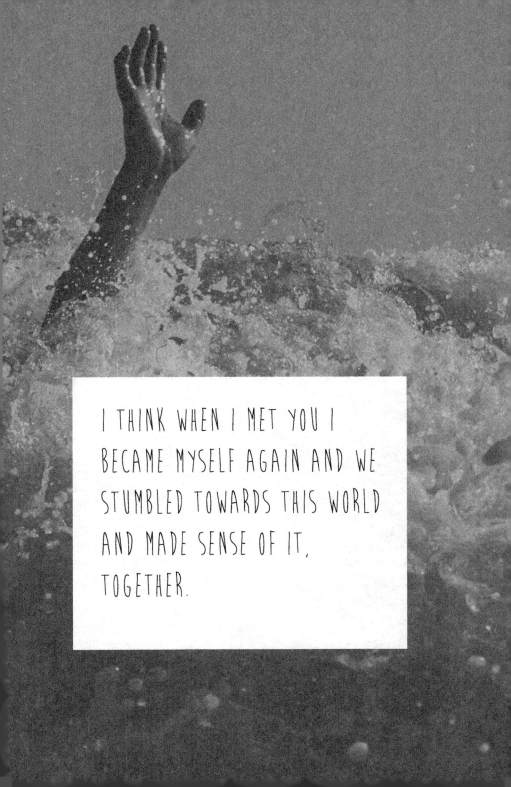

I THINK WHEN I MET YOU I
BECAME MYSELF AGAIN AND WE
STUMBLED TOWARDS THIS WORLD
AND MADE SENSE OF IT,
TOGETHER.

SUDDENLY I REMEMBERED THAT LAUGH, IT TOLD A DIFFERENT STORY, OUR STORY.

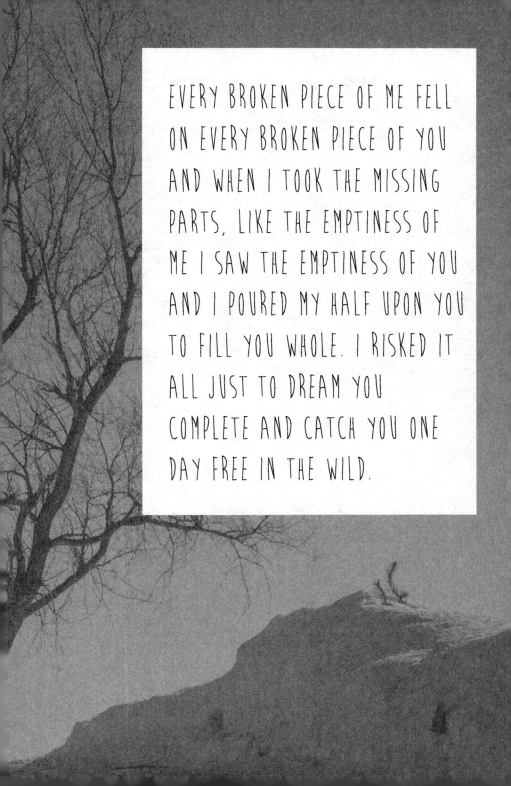

EVERY BROKEN PIECE OF ME FELL
ON EVERY BROKEN PIECE OF YOU
AND WHEN I TOOK THE MISSING
PARTS, LIKE THE EMPTINESS OF
ME I SAW THE EMPTINESS OF YOU
AND I POURED MY HALF UPON YOU
TO FILL YOU WHOLE. I RISKED IT
ALL JUST TO DREAM YOU
COMPLETE AND CATCH YOU ONE
DAY FREE IN THE WILD.

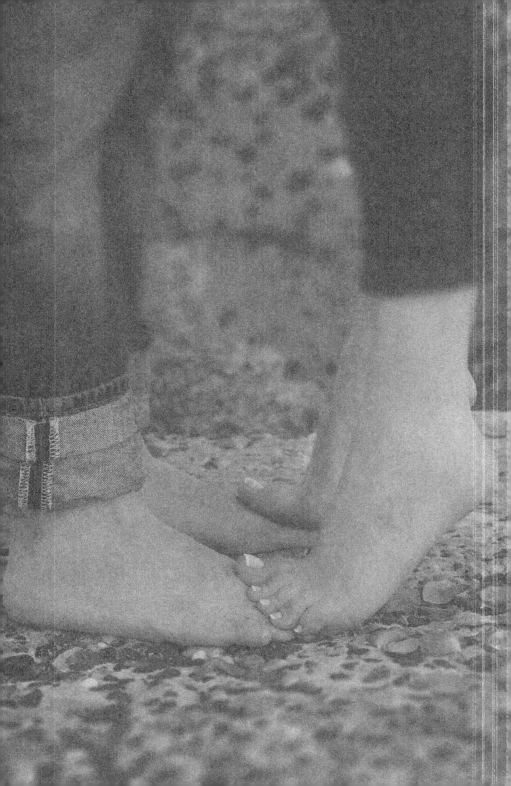

I WROTE HER STORY BECAUSE SHE
WANTED TO LIVE FOREVER AND I
LOVED HER FAR MORE WITH EVERY
WORD, TOO MUCH! EVEN IN DEATH
HER LIFE SOUGHT OUT BEAUTY,
FOR HER MOMENTS WERE
CONSUMED WITH LOVE AND I
COULD NEVER WRITE SUCH A
STORY WITHOUT HER STARS
FLAMING IN MY HEART.

MAYBE I HOPE TOO MUCH. MAYBE
I DREAM TOO MUCH. OR MAYBE
I LOVE TOO MUCH TO JUST GIVE
UP ON YOU.

MAYBE ALL THAT WE ARE IS WHAT PEOPLE EXPECT US TO BE.

EXCUSE ME, I FEEL INTERRUPTED AND I THINK I'VE OVERDOSE FROM THE IDEA OF LOVING YOU.

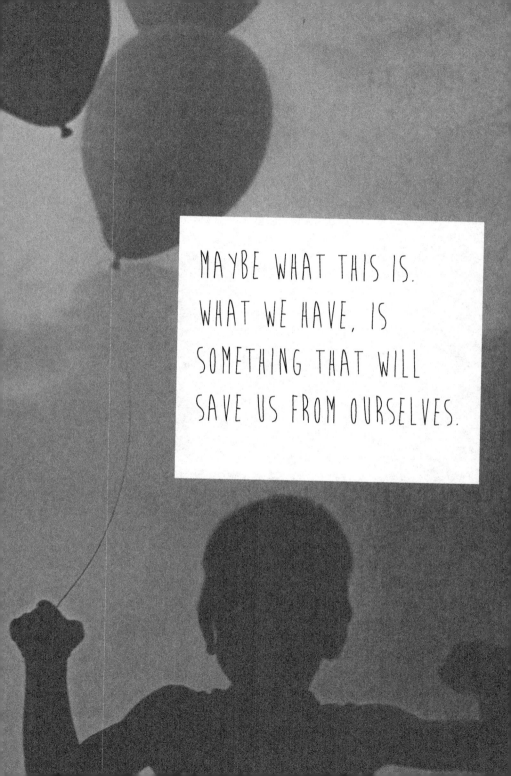

MAYBE WHAT THIS IS. WHAT WE HAVE, IS SOMETHING THAT WILL SAVE US FROM OURSELVES.

SHE WILDLY BURNED FOR THE
ONE SHE LOVED AND HE
STOOD THERE WATCHING,
HOPING HE TOO WOULD CATCH
A BLAZE FROM THE VIOLENCE
STIRRING IN HER HEART.

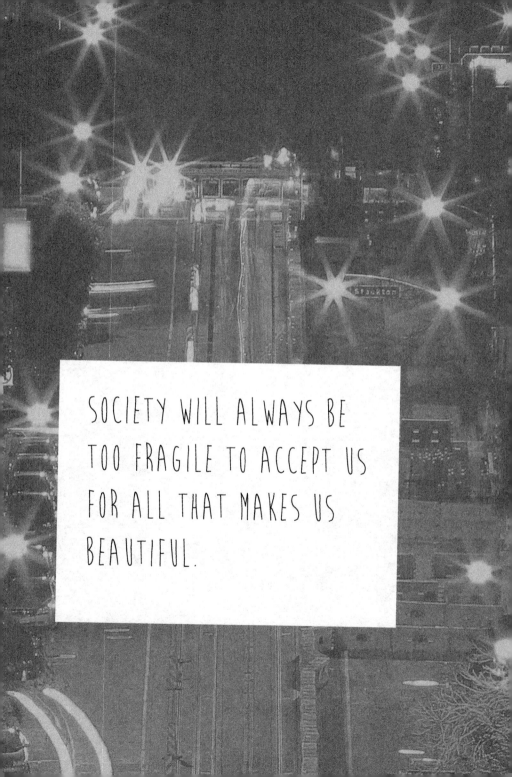

SOCIETY WILL ALWAYS BE
TOO FRAGILE TO ACCEPT US
FOR ALL THAT MAKES US
BEAUTIFUL.

I KNOW HOW YOU FEEL BECAUSE I'VE BEEN THERE TOO. I'VE HATED AND I'VE LOVED. I'VE SEEN MY DEMONS ROOT AND CRAWL AND MY ANGELS BRANCH AND SOAR. I'VE DIED WITHIN MYSELF AND LIVED A THOUSAND DIFFERENT LIVES. I TOO FIGHT THE SAME WAR AND I TOO AM DROWNING IN THE PUDDLES OF SELF-CONSCIOUSNESS THIS WORLD CREATED.

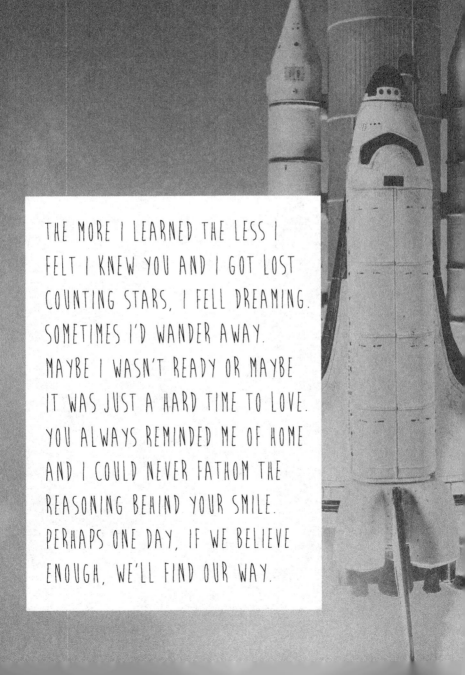

THE MORE I LEARNED THE LESS I
FELT I KNEW YOU AND I GOT LOST
COUNTING STARS, I FELL DREAMING.
SOMETIMES I'D WANDER AWAY.
MAYBE I WASN'T READY OR MAYBE
IT WAS JUST A HARD TIME TO LOVE.
YOU ALWAYS REMINDED ME OF HOME
AND I COULD NEVER FATHOM THE
REASONING BEHIND YOUR SMILE.
PERHAPS ONE DAY, IF WE BELIEVE
ENOUGH, WE'LL FIND OUR WAY.

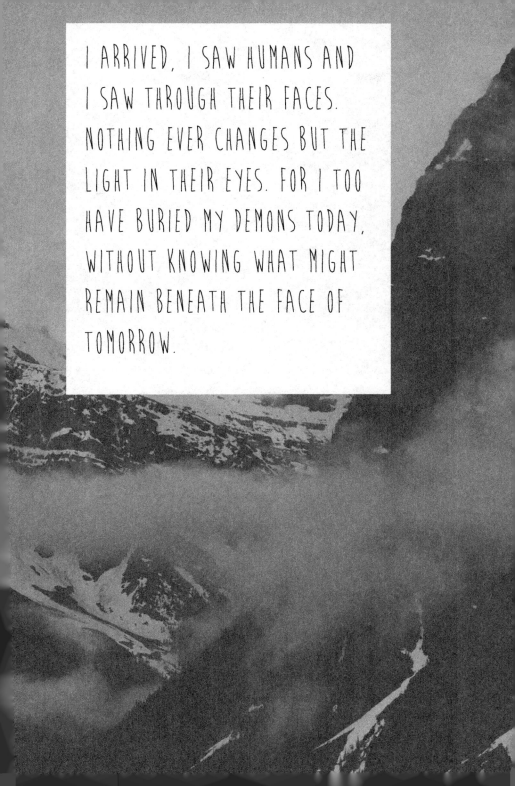

I ARRIVED, I SAW HUMANS AND I SAW THROUGH THEIR FACES. NOTHING EVER CHANGES BUT THE LIGHT IN THEIR EYES. FOR I TOO HAVE BURIED MY DEMONS TODAY, WITHOUT KNOWING WHAT MIGHT REMAIN BENEATH THE FACE OF TOMORROW.

IT'S DARK AND I'M
READING MY SCARS
BECAUSE OUR MOMENTS
REMIND ME OF WHERE
I SHOULD BE.

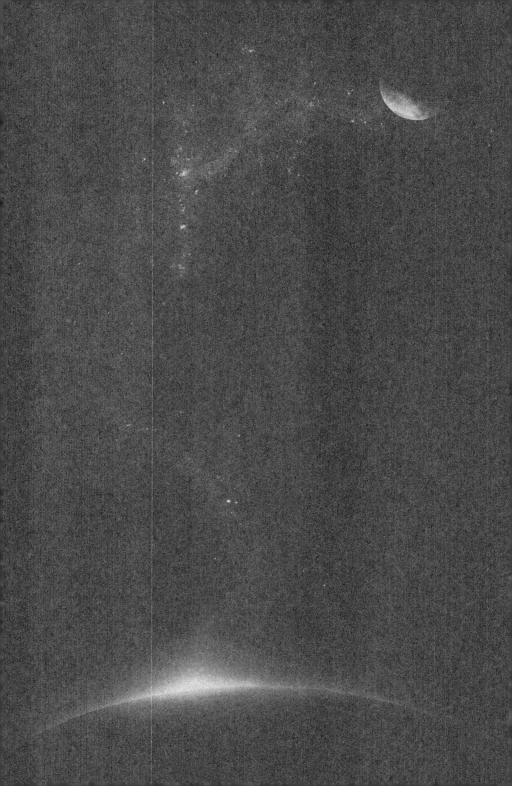

THE SEED OF OUR LOVE
WILL ALWAYS CUBE
WITHIN THE WONDER OF
INFINITE.

DEATH IS THE EASY PART, THE HARD PART IS LIVING AND KNOWING YOU COULD BE SO MUCH MORE THAN YOU'RE WILLING TO BE.

THE FEAR OF LOVING A
DOG, IS KNOWING ONE
DAY THEY'LL BE GONE
AND YOU COULD NEVER
FIND EYES THAT EXPRESS
ALL THAT YOU FEEL.

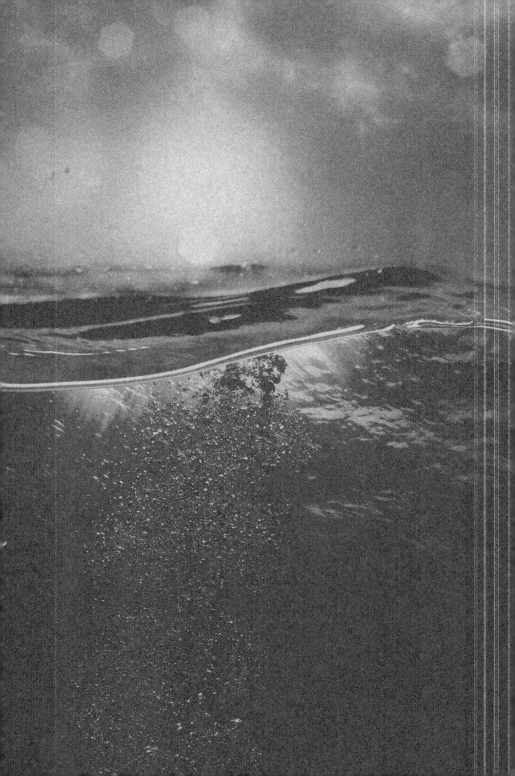

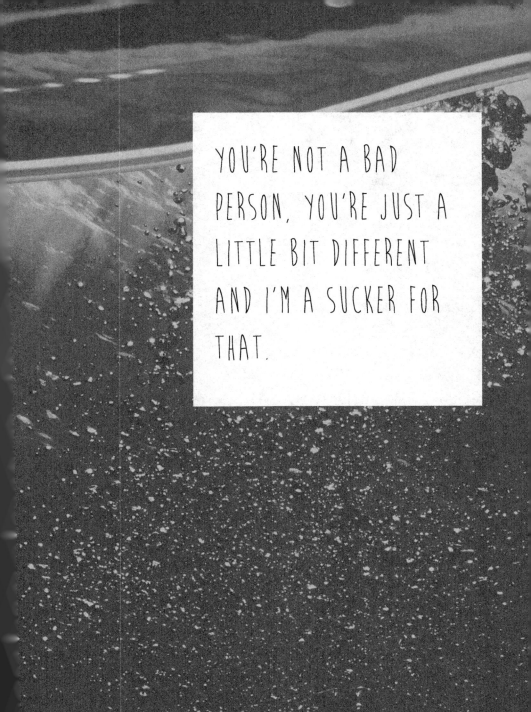

YOU'RE NOT A BAD PERSON, YOU'RE JUST A LITTLE BIT DIFFERENT AND I'M A SUCKER FOR THAT.

YOUR GREATEST DREAMS
WILL ALWAYS SLUMBER
WITHIN THE VICIOUS
DEPTHS OF FEAR.

SHE DREAMED IN COLOR
AND DESIGNED A WORLD
WHERE LOVE WAS
INEVITABLE.

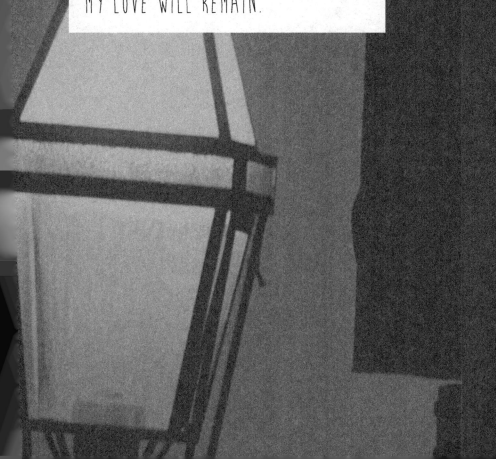

I'LL LOVE YOU WITH EVERY LITTLE
BIT OF EVERYTHING THAT HAS EVER
CONSUMED ME AND I WILL FOREVER
LOVE YOU AND FOREVER FIND YOU
IN EVERY LIFE TIME AND SO ON.
UNTIL THE STARS DIE OUT AND THE
UNIVERSE LEAPS BUT EVEN THEN,
MY LOVE WILL REMAIN.

SHE WAS BROKEN, I THINK IT'S BECAUSE SHE LOVED TOO MUCH AND SHE WAS ALWAYS BLIND TO THE FACT THAT LOVE TOO IS SOMETIMES BROKEN.

BRING ME BACK, SAVE ME
FROM ALL THAT I HAVE
BECOME. SAVE ME, JUST DO
IT! LET US BECOME THE
THINGS WE LOVE AND FIND
OUR WAY. LIKE WHEN THE
OCEAN IN YOUR EYES
REFLECT THE STARS IN MINE
AND LET THE DREAMS OF US
ALWAYS DRIFT TOWARDS THE
SHORES OF FOREVER.

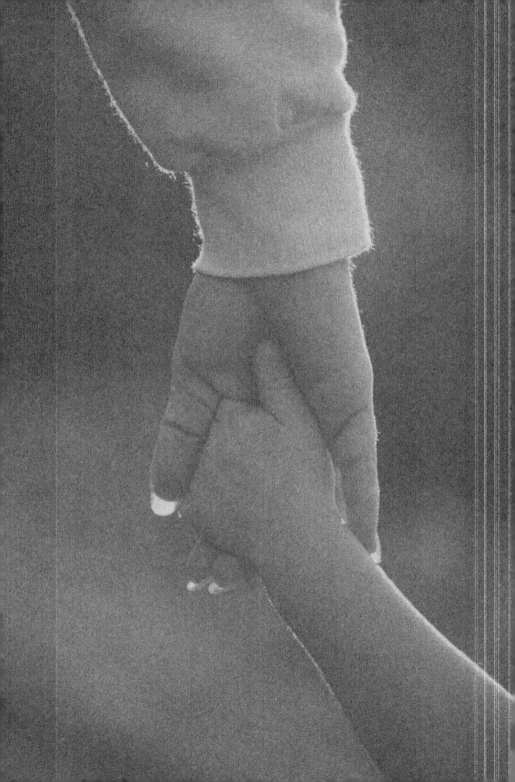

THE BEST KIND OF HUMANS,
ARE THE ONES WHO STAY.

SOMETIMES THOSE WE LOVE
BREAK US TO BIND US WHOLE
WITHIN THE TRANSITION.

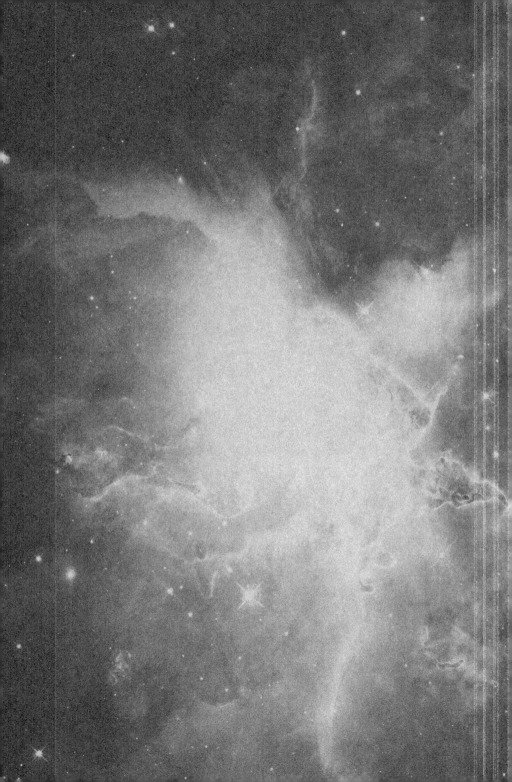

THE CHAOS IN ME IS THE CHAOS
IN YOU. LIKE THE LOVE IN YOU
IS THE LOVE IN ME. SO MAYBE
WE'RE BOTH A LITTLE CRAZY.
ENOUGH TO BELIEVE WE'RE
FOUND WHERE DREAMS ARE BORN
AND BENEATH OUR FAULTS
REMAIN A SCIENCE, WHERE YOU
AND I WILL RUN AWAY AND LEAVE
NOTHING BEHIND.

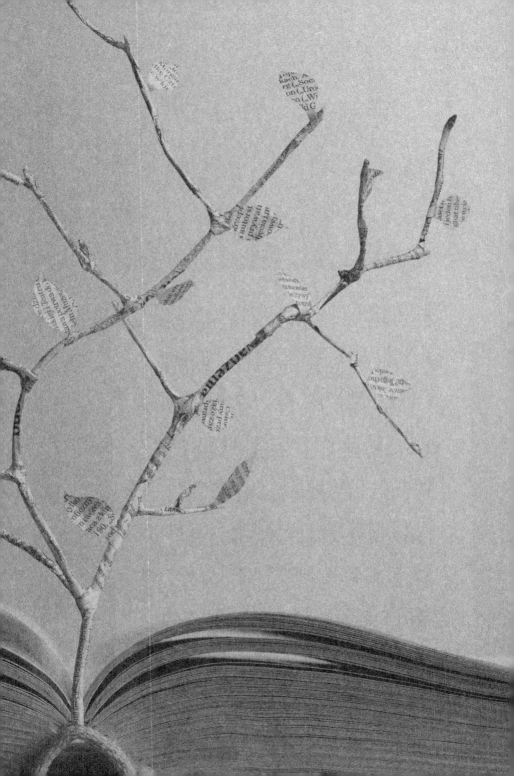

"IF YOUR WORDS COULD COME TO
LIFE IT WOULD BE THE MOST
BEAUTIFUL PERSON EVER."
SHE SAID.

"OH BUT MY DEAR, I AM MY
WORDS."
HE REPLIED.

BUT DEAR, DON'T BE AFRAID OF LOVE IT'S ONLY MAGIC.

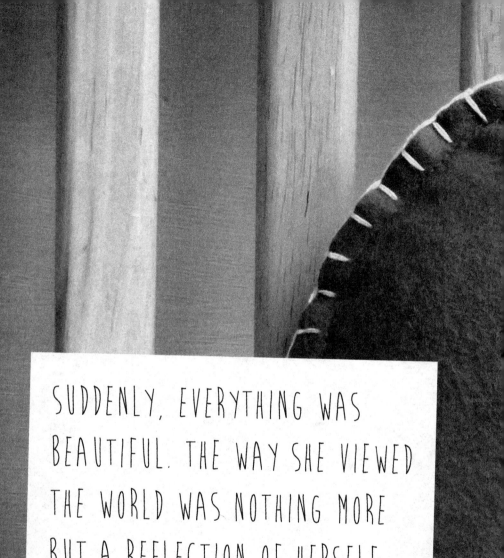

SUDDENLY, EVERYTHING WAS BEAUTIFUL. THE WAY SHE VIEWED THE WORLD WAS NOTHING MORE BUT A REFLECTION OF HERSELF.

IT'S FUNNY, FOR ALL IT TOOK
WAS A BROKEN HEART AND THAT
ALONE WAS ENOUGH, ENOUGH FOR
HER TO DO EVERYTHING SHE EVER
DREAMED OF.

OH DARLING, HOW THE STARS INSIDE ME BURN FOR YOU.

TO LOVE IS TO SOAR
IN THE WILD UNEXPECTEDLY.

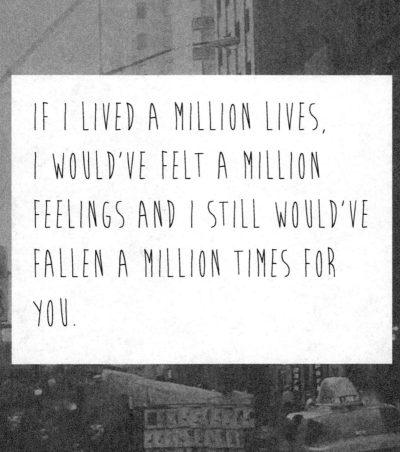

IF I LIVED A MILLION LIVES,
I WOULD'VE FELT A MILLION
FEELINGS AND I STILL WOULD'VE
FALLEN A MILLION TIMES FOR
YOU.

THIS LIFE, ALL THAT WE ARE,
EVERY DAY WE ARE CLOSER TO
OUR DOOM AND SOMEWHERE
BETWEEN LIFE AND DEATH, WE
MUST FIND THE SPACE OF ALL
THAT MAKES US SPECIAL.

SOMETIMES TO SELF-DISCOVER
YOU MUST SELF-DESTRUCT.

I HAD TO LEARN TO LIVE WITHOUT YOU AND I COULDN'T MAKE SENSE OF IT, BECAUSE I LEFT SO MUCH OF ME INSIDE OF YOU.

HOW COULD I LIVE ABOVE THE WATER OR BREATHE UNDER IT. HOW COULD I SWIM IN DARKNESS CONSUMED IN AN OCEAN OF YOU? FALLING OR FLYING TOWARDS YOU, LOSING OR FINDING MYSELF IN YOU AND BEAUTY WAS NEVER THE WORD TO CATCH ALL THAT YOU ARE. FOR NOW I KNOW THE MEANS OF THE INFINITE AND IT ALL STARTS AND ENDS WITH YOU.

TO BE HUMAN IS TO BE BROKEN AND BROKEN IS ITS OWN KIND OF BEAUTIFUL.

SOMEWHERE ALONG THE WAY WE ALL GO
A BIT MAD. SO BURN, LET GO AND DIVE
INTO THE HORROR, BECAUSE MAYBE IT'S
THE CHAOS WHICH HELPS US FIND WHERE
WE BELONG.

with open eyes, i see the world.
with an open heart i see the souls.
and with an open mind i see it all differently.

Thank you for your time.

Robert. M. Drake.

This book is dedicated to Charise. May her flame
live on within my heart and continue to inspire me
every waking hour.

ALSO AVALIABLE

ROBERT M. DRAKE
SPACESHIP

GRAVITY

A Novel by Robert M. Drake

Coming Soon...

Just a quick note,

I want to thank all of you for giving me the drive to make this book.

If it wasn't for all the support and love from all of you, this wouldn't be

possible. In short, I love you all for this and I love you all because all

of you inspire me to keep going and going. Remember all dreams are

possible only if you believe in them. Stay forever young,stay forever

beautiful.

CPSIA information can be obtained
at www.ICGtesting.com
Printed in the USA
FSOW04n2237020917
38088FS